People of the Bible

The Bible through stories and pictures

Moses
Leads His
People

Moses Leads His People

Retold by Catherine Storr
Pictures by Jim Russell

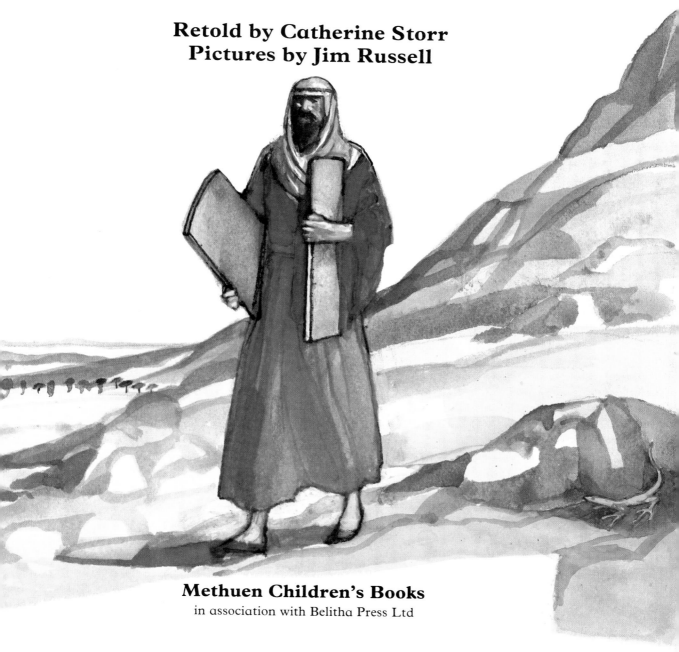

Methuen Children's Books
in association with Belitha Press Ltd

After the last of the plagues
which God had sent to the Egyptians,
Pharaoh told the Children of Israel
to leave Egypt as soon as they could.
They took jewels of gold and silver
from the Egyptians.
'Go quickly,' they said, 'or we shall all be dead men.'

The Israelites left at once.
They took their bread-dough with them
without waiting for it to rise,
so it was unleavened bread.
By day they followed a pillar of cloud,
and by night a pillar of fire.

After they had left,
Pharaoh's heart was hardened again.
He sent an army to bring them back to Egypt.

When the Children of Israel
saw Pharaoh's chariots pursuing them, they said,
'Were there no graves for us in Egypt?
You have led us out to die in the wilderness.'
But Moses said,
'Fear not. Keep still and God will save you.'

Moses stretched out his hand over the sea,
and God sent a strong east wind to blow all night.
In the morning, the sea parted and there was
dry land between two walls of water.
The Children of Israel went safely through.

But when the Egyptians followed,
Moses stretched out his hand again
and the waters returned
and rushed over the Egyptians.
Every man was drowned.

As they went on through the desert
the people became hungry.
They complained to Moses,
'In Egypt we had fleshpots and bread.
Here we shall die of starvation.'

Moses said, 'God has heard you complain.
He will give you meat to eat in the evening,
and bread in the morning.'
That evening the ground was covered with quails.

The next morning there was manna
scattered all over the camp.

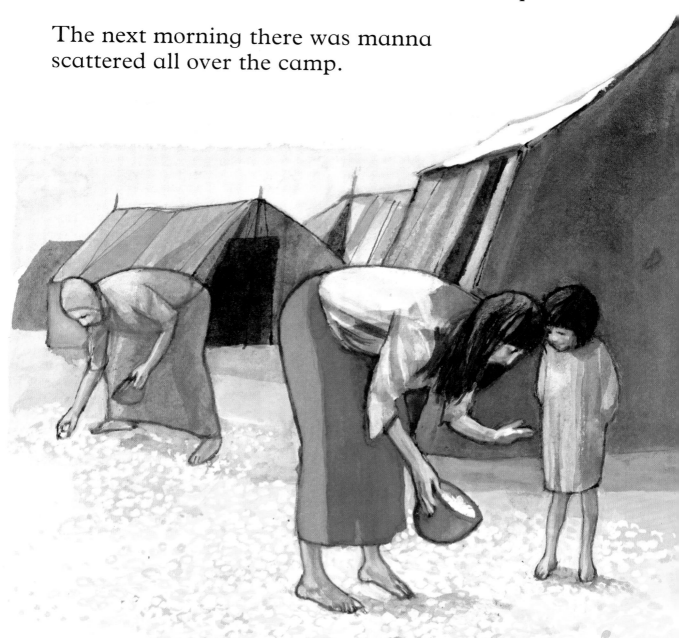

As the Israelites journeyed in the wilderness,
they found no water. They were very thirsty,
and they complained again to Moses.
God told Moses, 'Go and stand before the rock
of Horeb and strike it with your rod.
Then water will flow and my people shall drink.'

But now the Amalekites came to fight the Israelites.
Moses called Joshua, the son of Nun,
to lead the army.
'I will stand on that hill, with the rod of God
in my hand,' he said.
Sometimes one side won and sometimes the other.
Moses found that if he lifted up his hands
the Israelites were victorious.
If his hands fell down, the Amalekites won.
He sat on a stone, and Aaron and Hur
held up his hands for him,
until Joshua had won the battle.

After three months in the wilderness
the Children of Israel came to the desert of Sinai.
God called Moses up into the mountain.
He said, 'If my people obey my commandments,
they shall be a holy nation and my chosen people.
Go down and tell them to be ready for me
on the third day.'

On the third day there was thunder and lightning,
and a black cloud hung over the mountain.
The voice of the trumpet sounded.
The people trembled and the mountain quaked.
God said to Moses,
'Come up the mountain again,
and I will give you my laws.'

God gave these commandments for his people.
You shall have no other gods, but Me.
You shall not make idols.
You shall worship the Lord, the one God.
You shall not swear, nor steal, nor kill each other.
You must honour your fathers and mothers.
You shall not work on the Sabbath, the seventh day.
You shall not say wrong things about your neighbour,
nor try to steal his wife.
You shall not envy anything that belongs
to a neighbour – his land, or his cattle.
God wrote these laws on two tablets of stone.

Moses stayed on the mountain
for forty days and forty nights.
While he was gone, the people came to Aaron
and said, 'We don't know where Moses is,
or if he will ever come back.
Make us a god to lead us.'
So Aaron made a statue of a calf, all of gold.
He said, 'Here is your god. Worship him.'

On the mountain, God said to Moses,
'Go down to the people.
They are worshipping an idol instead of me.
I shall punish them.'
Moses said, 'Lord God, do not be angry
with your people.
Remember Abraham and Isaac and Jacob
and your promises to them.'

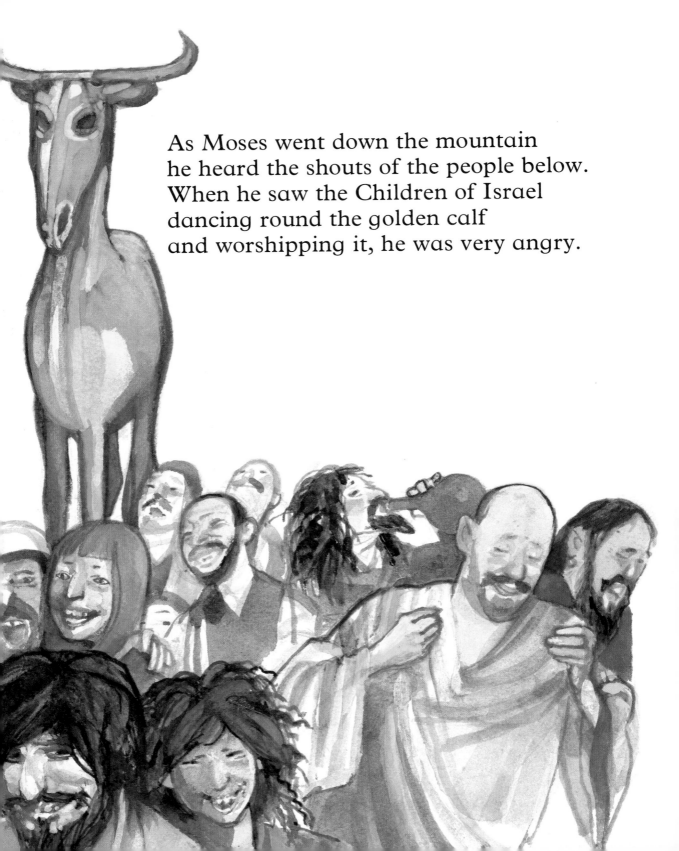

As Moses went down the mountain
he heard the shouts of the people below.
When he saw the Children of Israel
dancing round the golden calf
and worshipping it, he was very angry.

He threw the two stone tablets to the ground, and they broke into pieces.

Moses said to Aaron, 'What have the people done
to you that you should make them sin in this way?'
Aaron said, 'Don't be so angry.
The people meant no harm.
We did not know where you were,
so they asked me to make them a new god.'
Moses stood at the gate of the camp, and said,
'Whoever is on God's side, let him come to me here.'
All the sons of the tribe of Levi came to Moses' side.

Then Moses pleaded with God
to forgive the Children of Israel their sin
in making the golden calf.

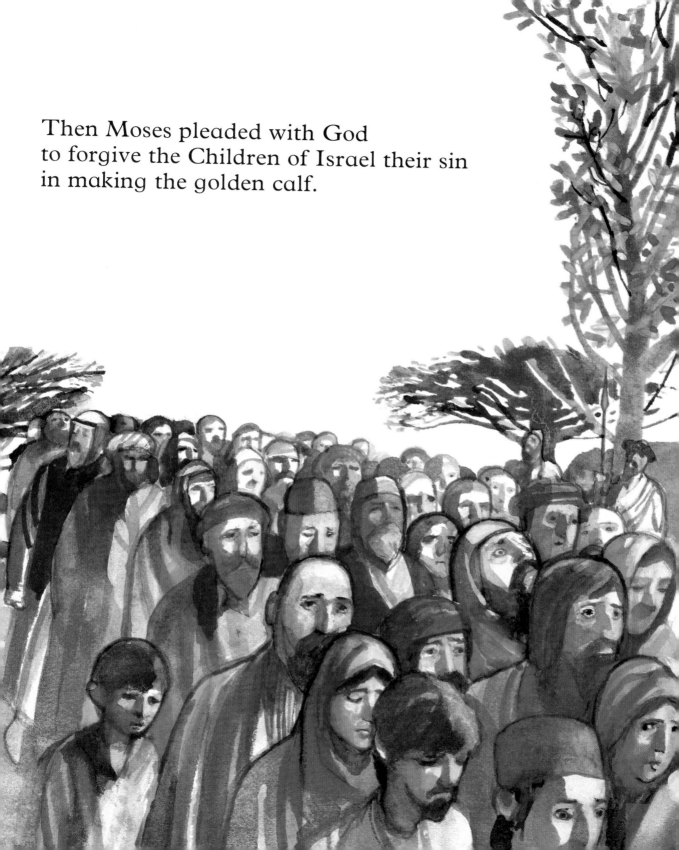

God said to Moses,
'Now, go on into the wilderness.
I will send an angel before you
and I will bring my people
into a land flowing with milk and honey.'
The people watching saw the pillar of cloud
and knew that God was speaking to Moses
as a friend.
Moses asked God, 'May I see your face in glory?'
God said, 'No. That would be too much for you.
Stand on a rock, and I will pass by,
and you will see a part of my glory.'

God told Moses to make two new tablets of stone.
He said, 'I will write my commandments on them.'
Early the next morning,
Moses went up to the top of Mount Sinai.
God told him to lead the Children of Israel
to live in Canaan.

When Moses came down from Mount Sinai
where he had been talking with God,
the skin of his face shone,
so that the people were afraid to come near him.

Now the fine craftsmen of the people
began to make the Tabernacle ready for the Ark.
The Tabernacle tent had curtains
of blue and purple and scarlet linen,
embroidered with golden cherubs.

Inside the Tabernacle tent was a box
made of acacia wood,
to hold the tablets of stone.
This was the Ark.
Aaron and his sons were the priests of the Tabernacle.
They made a burnt offering on the golden altar
and the glory of the Lord was over the Tabernacle.

The Desert Wanderings

Mt. Ararat

Tarshish

R. Tigris

Ninevah

R. Euphrates

Mediterranean Sea

Nazareth   *Sea of Galilee*

Joppa   Bethlehem

Jerusalem

Hebron   Canaan

Land of Goshen

WILDERNESS

Succoth

Bitter Lakes

Memphis   S I N A I

EGYPT

Mt Sinai/Horeb

Thebes

The exact place where the
Children of Israel crossed
the water and escaped from
the Egyptians is not known.
They might have crossed a
lake, or a narrow inlet of
the sea. Some scholars
think it might have been
called 'the Reed Sea' and
that over the years this was
muddled with 'the Red Sea'.